contents

introduction

It becomes the office of the educator to select those things within the range of existing experience that have the promise and potentiality of presenting new problems which by stimulating new ways of observation and judgement will expand the area of further experience.
J. Dewey,
Experience and Education.

Primary teachers develop a keen awareness of the potential for cross-curriculum enquiry to be found in their childrens interest in the world around them.

As well as the large scale topics and projects often undertaken in Primary classrooms, we suggest that themes perhaps on a smaller scale, and centring on everyday objects which can easily be brought together for display and study, can also provide a springboard for wide-ranging integrated study.

"Themes Familiar" presents such ideas and suggestions for study and research using everyday objects as starting points.

Each theme can be covered at any length, depending upon the interest generated and the time available, but sufficient information is included to enable each theme to be developed as a full scale area of study.

The photographs of displays suggest ideas for stimulating interest as well as examples of children's work, but all of them are made up with objects that should be readily available to most classes.

The book will be particularly valuable in the planning stages of a topic. It includes:

- a wide selection of ideas in many aspects of language work.

- suggestions for mathematics which include problem-solving and investigations, and which should relate to any maths scheme.

- science-based activities which incorporate work in design and technology.

- a wide range of art and craft ideas which readily lend themselves to the use of a variety of media, tools and equipment.

- P.E. and games ideas and, where appropriate, board games and more light-hearted challenges in the toys and games section.

- a number of computer programs. These were correct at the time of publication, but teachers will no doubt wish to add to the list.

- many ideas under environmental studies, including much that is either historically or geographically based. Again, teachers will want to add to these activities to take account of their particular environment.

- a section entitled "other areas for discussion and investigation" which suggests ideas for open-ended cross curriculum enquiry.

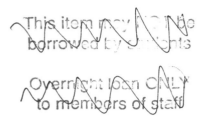

themes familiar

research and display in the primary school using everyday objects

Written by W. Booth, P. Briten and F. Scott
Illustrated by Lyn Gray

First published in 1987 by
Belair Publications Ltd.,
P.O. Box 12, Twickenham, England, TW1 2QL
© W. Booth, P. Briten and F. Scott, 1987
Cover design by James Hayworth
Design, setting and artwork by Solo Graphics
ISBN 0 947882 07 3

Printed and bound by Heanor Gate Printing Ltd, Heanor, Derbyshire.

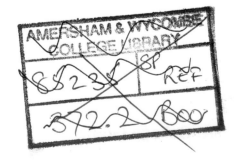

Pages 67 to 72 are set out to enable teachers to make their own additions to the text.

The authors have found that there can be a real sense of achievement and excitement amongst the children as they gradually discover that an object which they often take for granted can become the basis for wide-ranging study. Because of the unusual nature of the area under investigation, the resulting display work is also likely to be unusual; demanding by its very nature the inclusion of a variety of related objects and a lively three-dimensional display.

As teachers, the authors found they learnt a great deal as the topics included progressed. This sharing of learning with the children made the work interesting for teacher as well as pupil, and made research and investigation a natural as opposed to a contrived activity. We hope that you will share this excitement with your class as you pursue some of these topics.

Bill Booth
Paul Briten
Fenella Scott

balloons

DISCUSSION:
The different types of balloons (toy balloons, air balloons etc.)
Various uses for balloons, e.g. traffic control, travel, reconnoitring, scientific observation, warfare, meteorology.
The limitations of balloon travel.
Safety considerations with toy balloons.

LANGUAGE:

Writing:
- *Blown Away.* A balloon flight lands the passengers in an unexpected destination.
- Compose a cartoon story putting the dialogue into balloons. Make a balloonist's trip the subject of the story.
- Describe a balloonist's view of the school.
- *Free as Air.* A story of an escape by balloon.

Research:
Find out about: pilot balloon, captive balloon, barrage balloon, balloon, barrage, balloon fish, cartoon balloon, a dirigible, airship, Zeppelin, a blimp, weather balloon, balloon tyre.

Drama/Movement:
- The problem for a balloon seller with rather too many gas filled balloons.
- A balloon with a label, let off at the school fete results in the finder returning the balloon in person. Select an unusual character for the finder, and act out the scene.

7

Vocabulary:
Ascent, descent, aeronautics, gas, hydrogen, helium, inflate, deflate, jet-propulsion, propel, rubber, expand, ballast, stretch, soar, balloonist, jettison, altitude.
How many words can you find to rhyme with 'balloon'?

Stories:
The Red Balloon, Lamorisse, Unwin.
Around the World in Eighty Days, Jules Verne, Hippo Books
Let the Balloon Go, Ivan Southall, Puffin.

Poetry:
'in just', e.e. cummings in *Happenings,* Harrup & Co.
'who knows if the moon's a balloon', e.e. cummings in *Bulls Eyes,* Longman.
'Balloons', Sylvia Plath in *Bulls Eyes,* Longman.
'Balloons', Judith Thurman in *A First Poetry Book,* Oxford University Press.
'The Orange Balloon', Stanley Cook, *A Fourth Poetry Book,* Oxford University Press.
'The Balloons', Oscar Wilde in *The Oxford Books of Verse for Juniors, Book 4,* Oxford University Press.
'The Balloon Man', Rose Fyleman in *Passport to Poetry: Book 2,* Cassell.

MATHEMATICS:

How long can an inflated balloon be kept in the air without using hands or arms? Draw a graph of the class results.

Estimate and then measure the weight of water that can be held in a balloon.

A modern airship has an average cruising speed of 350 miles per hour. At this speed, approximately how long would it take to travel from the school to London, Manchester, etc?

Work out the direction the wind would need to blow in order for a balloon released in school to travel to New York, Moscow, Rome etc.

Work out the minimum weight required to prevent a gas-filled toy balloon from taking off.

Use a felt tipped pen to draw geometric shapes on a deflated balloon. Investigate how the shapes change when the balloon is inflated.

What is the fewest number of balloons you need to burst to score 30? Can you score 42 by bursting 3 balloons?
What is the (a) highest (b) lowest score you can achieve by bursting 5 balloons?

SCIENCE, DESIGN & TECHNOLOGY:

Pick up a teacup with a balloon: Partially blow up the balloon. Place the balloon on the rim of the cup and blow up the balloon a little more. This will reduce the air pressure inside the cup and it will stay attached to the balloon.

Jet propulsion.

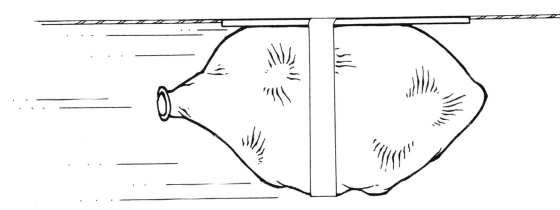

Balloon attached to drinking straw.

Make a hot air balloon with tissue paper. Launch the balloon in the open air with the teacher using a solid fuel heat source. Experiment with different shapes of balloon.

What causes a balloon to lift into the air?

Investigate how a balloon pump works.

Charge a balloon with electricity by rubbing it on a woollen garment. See how it sticks to wall or ceiling, or attracts pieces of paper or a trickle of water from the tap.

ART/CRAFT:

Hot air balloons are often imaginatively decorated. Design and cut out individual balloons, mount them on a *blue sky* background, and mount balloon poems or descriptions on the balloon baskets.

Draw or paint designs on deflated balloons. View them when the balloons are inflated.

Decorate inflated balloons.

Make a balloon rocket.

With a balloon as a base, use papier mâché to make large puppet heads, helmets or masks.

Design a television test card, showing the different shades and colours in different balloons.

Balloon sculpture. Twist and link together long narrow balloons to create an animal.

Design a pattern for curtain material or wallpaper, incorporating a balloon motif.

Balloon-nosed animals. Children paint and cut out large animals. An inflated balloon is attached as a nose using a drawing pin.

9

COMPUTER PROGRAMS:	*Air Balloons* [Mastermaths Series, Oxford University Press.] *Ballooning* [Five Ways Software, Heinemann.]

MUSIC: Blow up a balloon and by pinching the neck try to play a tune.

ENVIRONMENTAL STUDIES:

By making and using an anemometer and a wind direction finder, try to work out where a balloon would be (a) one hour (b) five hours after being released from the school playground.

Tie return labels to gas filled balloons. Use weather charts to guess where the balloons will fly when released. On a map, locate the places where the balloons are retrieved, and work out the distances of these locations from your school.

Investigate the purpose and use of meteorological balloons.

Find out about: (a) The Montgolfiers and the history of hot-air ballooning. (b) Count von Zeppelin (c) The history of airship flight. A useful source book is *Airships and Balloons* by Carey Miller. Pan Books.

Barrage balloons as used in the Second World War.

TOYS AND GAMES: Design a variety of pencil and paper and party games. (e.g. Tangled Strings, in which balloons have to be matched to their owners, balloon tennis, balloon volleyball, etc.)

VISITS: An aeronautical museum.

OTHER AREAS FOR DISCUSSION AND INVESTIGATION:

Use *The Guinness Book of Records* to discover:
  (a) The record distance travelled by a balloon.
  (b) The highest altitude achieved by a balloon (manned and unmanned).
  (c) The greatest number of toy balloons released at one time.
  (d) The longest recorded flight of a toy balloon.

Balloons are supported by air. Consider other objects that require air for support, e.g. lifejackets, tyres, swimming rings.

bicycles

DISCUSSION:

When are bicycles more useful than cars?
Different kinds of bicycles and their uses.
Bicycle safety and the Highway Code.
BMX bicycles and cycling tricks.

LANGUAGE:

Writing:
- *Let down by a puncture* – stranded in the worst possible place.
- Describe the functions of different parts of a bicycle, e.g. brakes, pump, chain, handlebars etc.
- Write instructions for a beginner on how to use and care for a bicycle.

Research:
Find out about: tandem, unicycle, tricycle, hobby-horse, velocipede, boneshaker, sprocket, dynamo, Moulton, penny-farthing, chopper, *wheelie*, exercise bike.

Drama/Movement:
- Mime riding on a unicycle, a tandem.
- Mime Blondin cycling on a highwire across Niagara Falls.

Vocabulary:
- Stabilizers, saddle, frame, handlebars, mudguards, reflector, dynamo, lamps, tyres, pedals, gears, brakes, chain, cyclometer, ball-bearings, pannier, accessories, cog, puncture, hub.
- *Cycle* comes from a Greek word *kyklos* meaning a circle or a wheel. Find other words beginning with *cyclo* and their meanings.

Stories:
Queen's Nose, Dick King-Smith, Puffin Books.
The New Bike and Other Stories, Simon Watson, Young Puffins.

'Esme on her Brother's Bicycle', Russell Hoban, *Delights and Warnings,* Macdonald.
'Going Downhill on a Bicycle: A Boy's Song', Henry Charles Beeching, in *Out of School Anthology,* Evans Pub.
'The Fate of an Icycle' by Alan Sillitoe in *A Second Poetry Book,* OUP.
'Racing Cyclist', Stanley Cook, in *A Fifth Poetry Book,* OUP.

MATHEMATICS:

Make a study of shapes on a bicycle.

How many times will the wheels turn when a bicycle travels 1 km?

Speed – work out speeds in km/hr from a measured ride in the school grounds.

Prepare line graphs based on a bicycle journey.

Cost of bicycles – a survey.

Time a variety of manouevres and activities carried out on bicycles in the school playground – e.g. completing an obstacle course around skittles. Make graphical representation of results.

Statistics – survey the different makes of bicycle belonging to children in class/school.

Measure with a cyclometer.

What is a cycloid? Draw a cycloid by plotting on paper using a coin or circular disc, or on a playground wall using a bicycle wheel and chalk.

Number 'Wheel and Spokes' puzzle:

Each spoke and each outer wheel section is made up of three numbers all adding up to the same total. Find this number as well as all the missing numbers.

On a blank Number Wheel arrange the numbers 1 to 19 so that the twelve sections each add up to 22.

SCIENCE, DESIGN & TECHNOLOGY:

(see *Things That Go*, Usborne Publishing Ltd.)

Why do cycle race-tracks have steep banking?

How could a bicycle be used to wind a ball of string? Think of other jobs a bicycle could do. Illustrate your ideas.

Design and make or draw devices for keeping you dry when cycling in the rain.

Set up a practical situation when a leak in a bicycle inner tube can be located and repaired in the classroom.

Find out how a cycle dynamo produces electricity.

How long can you balance in a still position on a bicycle with both feet off the ground? Carry out a test with different people. What can you discover about the principles of stability?

Study the purpose of ball-bearings in a wheel hub.

Investigate the effect of linking different-sized cog wheels. (Use lego-technik equipment or the computer programme *COGS*).

'Bicycle Paradox' — Tie a rope to the lower pedal of a bicycle and, with someone holding the bike upright, pull backwards on the rope. Does the bike move backwards, forwards or not at all?

Design (a) an anti-theft device for your bicycle.
      (b) a multi-purpose bag (pannier) for carrying shopping etc. on a bicycle.
      (c) a special bicycle for a postman (see Edward de Bono *Children Solve Problems*, Penguin).

ART/CRAFT:

Draw your bicycle from memory, and then from close observation.

Discuss the similarities and differences between the two drawings.

Draw a part of a bicycle from close observation. Underneath your drawing write a description of its function.

Design and draw a bicycle of the future.

Make a bicycle collage using, for example, milk straws for the frame, string for the chain, pipe cleaners for the handlebars, matchsticks for the pedals.

Draw different perspectives of a bicycle.

Draw the back-marker's view of the Tour de France Cycle Race.

Design a poster promoting the use and sale of bicycles.

Design a safety poster for cyclists.

Take a wheel shape. Fill each division with a different pattern.

Using modeller's wire, make a penny-farthing bicycle model.

Prepare a wall time-frieze showing the history of the bicycle.

COMPUTER PROGRAMS:	*Cogs* (Newman College) *Cycle* (Newman College) *Bike* (Clywd Technics Road Safety Programme)
MUSIC:	'Daisy Bell', Ta-ra-ra boom-de-ay. A. & C. Black.
ENVIRONMENTAL STUDIES:	The earliest bicycles did not have — brakes, gears, dynamos, pneumatic tyres, bells. Find out how each feature has improved the bicycle. Use a suitable map to plan a cycle tour in your locality to visit its main historical/geographical features. What distance would you travel? How long might your cycle trip take? Plan some interesting cycling routes in your local area designed to take (a) 30 minutes (b) 1 hour (c) 2 hours (d) 4 hours (e) 10 hours. Plan and cost a cycling tour (a) in this country (b) abroad. History and development of the bicycle. Find out which countries have more bikes than cars. Why should this be? Find out about the Tour de France — route, personalities, records.
P.E./GAMES:	Slow bicycle races Bicycle obstacle races Cyclo-Cross BMX Competitions Bicycle football — perhaps 5-a-side on the school field.
VISITS:	Transport section of a Museum. Ask your local police or road safety officer to visit the school to discuss road safety. Try to arrange some cycle training for all cyclists in the school. A bicycle shop — perhaps to see repairs being carried out.
OTHER AREAS FOR DISCUSSION AND INVESTIGATION:	Have a bicycle displayed upside down in the classroom to prompt discussion and investigation. Investigate the many national and world cycling records (speed, distance, duration) as given in *The Guinness Book of Records.* Find out about the great variety of bicycle accessories, cycle maintenance kits and repair kits. Find out about folding bicycles, the Milk Race, and circus cycle acts (unicycles, high wire cycling). Investigate clothes for cycling by day, at night, in wet weather, in hot countries. Make a survey of current cycling magazines and publications.

THE HOBBY-HORSE
1819

THE PENNY-FARTHING
1870

THE MOTORAD
1896

THE CHOPPER
1970

bottles

DISCUSSION:
The advantages and disadvantages of using glass bottles for storage.
The different types of bottle used in the home.
Alternatives to glass bottles for storage.
The need for conserving and re-cycling glass products.

LANGUAGE:

Writing:
- A *genie in a bottle* story;
- An adventure arising from the discovery of a message in a bottle.
- Psalm 56 refers to a 'tear-bottle' (a bottle for collecting tears). Write a story or poem based on finding a tear bottle.

Research:
Find out about: bottle-chart, bottle fish, bottle-head whale, bottle-nose dolphin, bottle-neck, bottle-gas, bottle-shouldered, bottle-imp, bottle-tree, smelling-bottle, bottle panes, bottle-glass, bottle-fed, bottle bank, hot-water bottles, soda syphon, cullet, flagon, decanter, pottle, silica.

Drama/Movement:
- Create scenes in which you attempt to persuade people (e.g. parents, hotelier, shopkeeper) to use a bottle-bank.
- Children become bottles containing different liquids. Develop some amusing conversations. (Experiment with ways of producing bottle-pouring sound effects.)

Vocabulary:
Cork, stopper, corkscrew, contents, crate, label, cylinder, glass, engraved, embossed, liquid, pour. 'Bottle' as a noun and as a verb.

Phrases and sayings:
To bottle up one's feelings; to have a lot of bottle; chief cook and bottle-washer; to put new wine into old bottles.

Stories:
Genie in a bottle stories
'The Old Woman Who Lived in a Vinegar Bottle' Dorothy Edwards from *The Magician Who Kept a Pub,* Fontana.

Poetry:
'15 men on the dead man's chest,
Yo-ho-ho, and a bottle of rum!
Drink and the devil had done for the rest —
Yo-ho-ho, and a bottle of rum!'
Treasure Island: R. L. Stevenson

'Shake and shake the ketchup bottle.
None will come and then a lot'll.'

MATHEMATICS:

Find 4 bottles with similar capacities. Devise a method of determining which bottle has (a) the smallest, and (b) the greatest capacity without using a calibrated measure.

Discover a method of finding the surface area of a wine or milk bottle.

How many one pint milk bottles are used in a year by (a) one family, (b) all the families in the class or school?

Fill a bottle with marbles. Work out a method of estimating, as accurately as possible, the number of marbles in the bottle.

Use milk crates and wine racks for number operation exercises.

Set a tap running slowly. Estimate how long it would take to fill a litre bottle. Use a litre bottle and a stop watch or timer to check the accuracy of your estimate. At this rate of flow, how much water would come from the tap in (a) one day (b) one week?

SCIENCE, DESIGN & TECHNOLOGY:

Make a 'ship in a bottle'. Devise a method for erecting the mast.

How much air can you exhale in one breath? Place a straw or tube into water. Blow through it so that the expired air forces out the water from an inverted wide-neck bottle placed in a bowl of water.

Make a bottle-garden in a large narrow necked bottle.

Design and make a milk-bottle holder to take up to four bottles which has an indicator to order the day's milk and a device to prevent birds pecking the bottle tops.

Make a 5-minute timer from a plastic bottle. Use a transparent plastic bottle, with its base cut off, inverted in a jar. Fill the inverted bottle with water and make a small hole in its lid to allow the water to drip through.

Mark the jar with numbered labels at one-minute intervals.

'Egg in a Bottle' puzzle: a peeled hard-boiled egg will not go through the neck of a milk-bottle unless a few burning matches are placed in the bottle first.

Investigate the evaporation of liquid from bottles of different shape, volume and neck-size. Use the same amount of liquid in each bottle to compare rates of loss.

How much water can be put into a screw topped bottle before it sinks?

ART/CRAFT: Decorate a bottle to make an attractive candle-holder.

Look at green glass. Carry out paint-mixing exercises to create a bottle-green colour match. Paint, using bottle-green as the basic colour.

Study and draw distortions created by looking through glass bottles.

Make a bottle-cover in knitted wool, macramé, material with an appliqué design, etc.

Model papier mâché on a bottle base to create bottle-people.

Use bottles as the base for making dolls dressed in different national costume.

Draw or paint a still-life of bottle arrangements.

Bottle-roller printing: glue string, fabric, leather, card etc. onto the surface of a bottle. Use this as a printing roller to create patterns and designs on paper or fabric.

Design and draw a bottle label for a particular product.

COMPUTER PROGRAMS:
Jars Acornsoft (estimating volumes of liquids)
Bottles (ITMA Shell) *Teaching with a Micro: Maths 2*
Jugs (SMILE — the First 31) (MEP-Capital Region) (Capacity problems)

MUSIC:
Make a bottle xylophone: create a musical scale by putting varying amounts of water into glass bottles. Compose a tune.
'Ten Green Bottles' (traditional) and its variant:-
'Ten bluebottles on a piece of meat' (repeat)
'And if one bluebottle should wipe its dirty feet,
Then next Sunday's dinner would not be fit to eat.'

ENVIRONMENTAL STUDIES:
The history of glass and bottle making.
Shaping bottles by glass-blowing and by moulding.
Glass re-cycling projects — bottle banks and the re-cycling process.
Make a collection of different bottles. Categorise these by use, shape, colour, size. (Include miniature bottles).
How were liquids stored and carried before the introduction of glass bottles.
What are the raw materials from which glass is made?
Make a study of bottle labels. What information do they contain?

GAMES:
Bottle stall — numbered bottles to be won in a lottery.
Fishing for bottles — with rod and line and curtain-ring hooks.
Spinning the bottle — whoever it points to wins a prize or pays a forfeit.

VISIT:
Glassworks, dairy, local supermarket, chemists, museums.

OTHER AREAS FOR DISCUSSION AND INVESTIGATION:

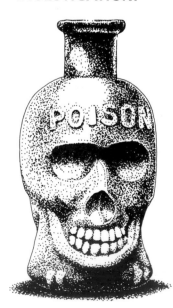

Bottle collection competition — how many different objects can be collected in a bottle?
Other interesting collections can be made of bottle tops, stoppers, corks, lids. Bottle openers, corkscrews etc. are also fascinating objects to collect and study.
Use *The Guinness Book of Records* to discover:-
    (a) The longest time taken for a message in a bottle to be found.
    (b) The largest bottle made and the smallest bottle on sale.
Where do corks come from? How can they be removed safely from bottles?
Why do some chemists have large long-necked bottles on display containing coloured liquids?

boxes

DISCUSSION:

When and why do we use boxes?
Different materials used for making boxes.
Different types of boxes.
Bring a box into the classroom. What's inside? Play a guessing game.

LANGUAGE:

Writing:
- *The Muddle* — Police are following two identical boxes, one of which contains smuggled weapons. The other contains Kim Taylor's birthday present.
- *Buried Treasure.*

Research:
Find out about: theatre box, post box, horse box, witness box, sentry box, box junction, Christmas box, box bed, box spanner, box office, box pleat, box room, Boxing Day, Box and Cox, Jack-in-the-Box, box wood, gear box, grass box, box camera, matchbox, gift box, cash box, box girder, snuff box, collecting box, box coat, soap box, penalty box, six yard box.

Drama/Movement:
- *Jack-in-the Box scenes* — someone opens the box — doll pops up and comes to life.
- Enact scenes based on a present being given.

Vocabulary:
Container, cuboid, rigid, capacity, flap, interior, exterior, volume, collapsible, packing, corrugated.

19

Stories:
Pandora's Box, Greek myth.
The Box of Delights, John Masefield, Fontana.
The Tinder Box, Hans Christian Andersen.
The Dead Letter Box, Jan Mark, Young Puffin Books.

Poetry:
'Window Boxes' by Eleanor Farjeon in *Poetry Plus Book 4*, Schofield & Sims.
'The Mutinous Jack-in-the-Box' by John Cunliffe in *A Second Poetry Book*, Oxford University Press.
'The Musical Box' by James Reaves in *The Wandering Moon*, Heinemann.

Sayings:
Watching the box, box in, boxing ears, box clever.

MATHEMATICS:

The shape of boxes — which shapes are good for packing?

A triangle is a strong shape — why are so few boxes triangular?

Make an open top box from one sheet of thin card (A4 size) to contain as much rice/sand as possible. Allow either sellotape or glue for flaps. (Suitable for class competition).

Capacities of different shaped boxes.

A study of faces, corners and edges.
Empty boxes: $4 + \square = 15$

How many right angles can be found on a box?

Study surface area.

Study the effect on the capacity of a box when length or breadth or height is increased.

Investigate the different ways a cube can be halved. (Use plasticine).

What is the smallest number of colours required to paint the faces of a cuboid so that all adjacent colours are different?

How many different pentominoes can be found to form open boxes?
How many different hexominoes can be found to form closed boxes?

SCIENCE, DESIGN & TECHNOLOGY:

Design and make boxes for packing various objects (consider hinged lids).

Design and make an interesting chocolate box which opens in an unusual way.

Study the workings of a box camera.

Design, make and fly a box kite.

Consider the construction and strength of a variety of boxes.

Design and make as strong a box as you can from given materials. The box is to contain a glass object. How much weight can be dropped on the box before it is crushed? (Suitable for class competition).

Devise a strength test for cardboard boxes — use your test on a variety of boxes.

Design a Jack-in-the Box.
Design and make a bird's nesting box.

Design and make a nest of boxes.

Boiling water in a paper box. *The Book of Experiments*, Leonard de Vries, John Murray.

ART/CRAFT:

Design and make a presentation box for a piece of jewellery.

Design and draw the cover for a cake or sweet box — including the side flaps.

Box modelling (e.g. Totem pole, robot, visitor from another planet).

Make a toy theatre from a cardboard box.

Design and make a doll's house.

Make a trinket box from self-hardening clay or papier mâché The lid should have an inset lip to hold it in position, and a padded interior.

Use different techniques, e.g. stencilling, relief painting, marbling, to decorate plain boxes.

Experiment with the cubists' approach to painting (Braque, Picasso).
Use a box to make a diorama of a scene, e.g. underwater, space or farm.

COMPUTER PROGRAMS:

Boxes and *Boxed, (SMILE — the First 31* M.E.P. Capital Region)
Build (M.E.P. Microprimer — Pack 3)
Raybox (M.E.P.)
The Music Box (Selective Software)
Box of Treasures (4-mation Software)

MUSIC:

'Little Boxes', *Alleluya*, A. & C. Black.
Make a sound box by stretching different sizes of elastic band over an open top box.
Make a double base using a tea chest, broom handle and string.

ENVIRONMENTAL STUDIES: Try to discover how many boxes are used by local traders, how they are delivered, and what happens to the boxes afterwards.
How are cardboard boxes made?
Study the markings on cardboard boxes. Try to work out where each box has come from.
Box the compass (say the compass points in the right order).
History and development of (a) pillar boxes (b) Jack-in-the Boxes.
Styles and designs of house letter boxes — a local survey.

P.E./GAMES: Give a name to each box on a badminton court or a netball court. e.g. North, South, East, West, A, B, C and D. When a box name is called the last person to stand in that box is out. The command "freeze!" when the last person is also out, will add to the fun.
Use of the P.E. "box".

TOYS/GAMES: Make up word boxes, e.g. names:

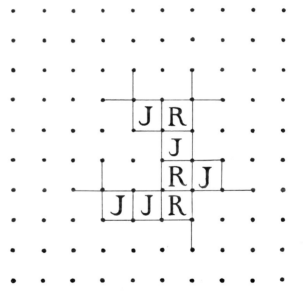

Children join dots to complete boxes.

How many different items can you collect in a match box? (Competition)

Rubik's Cube.

VISITS: The packaging department of any local factory. A box-making factory.

OTHER AREAS FOR DISCUSSION AND INVESTIGATION: Box numbers for newspaper advertisement replies.
Collect a variety of boxes. Discuss whether each box gave a clear impression of what it contained, or whether it was misleading. Discuss relevance of shape and sizes of boxes.
Why are boxes usually cuboids?

bricks

DISCUSSION: The reasons for building with different materials — at different times and in different places.
Bricks have different shapes, sizes, colours and surface-texture. Discuss the reasons for this.

LANGUAGE:

Writing:
- As the inventor of the brick, write a letter to explain/describe your invention and how it can be used to build a wall.
- Follow up a visit to a local building site with creative writing in prose and verse.

Research:
Find out about some of the following:-
air brick, damp course, cavity wall, mortar, bond, a brickbat, stretchers and headers, scaffolding, the 'frog' on a brick, fletton facing bricks.

Drama/Movement:
Act out the story of *The Three Little Pigs* or *The Selfish Giant.*

Vocabulary:
Vocabulary associated with brickbuilding, e.g. brickwork, hod, trowel, horizontal, vertical, chisel.

Phrases and Sayings:
To drop a brick, to make bricks without straw, You're a brick, banging one's head against a brick wall, like a ton of bricks.

Stories:

Three Little Pigs. Traditional and in Roald Dahl's *Revolting Rhymes* – Picture Puffin.

The Selfish Giant by Oscar Wilde, Cartoon version and in Picture Puffin.

'The Yellow Brick Road' in *The Wizard of Oz*, Frank L. Baum, Collins.

Poetry:

'There's a Red Brick Wall' by Nancy Chambers in *Poetry Plus: Book 3*, Schofield & Sims

'The Chimney' by Keith Bosley in *A Fourth Poetry Book*, O.U.P.

MATHEMATICS:

Estimate and then calculate accurately the number of bricks needed to build a wall of given dimensions (a) in lego; and (b) on site.

Calculate as accurately as possible the surface area of a brick. Remember to allow for any indentation.

Investigate the different tessellating patterns of rectangular bricks. Squared paper will be helpful for horizontal and vertical patterns. Include herring-bone as well.

Study of cuboids — parallel lines, corners, faces, edges, right angles, tessellations.

How does a bricklayer make sure his wall is vertical/horizontal? Investigate the use of a plumb line/spirit level.

Estimate the weight of a brick, then measure this accurately. Find the difference between the estimate and the measure.

Lower a brick into water. Discover its volume by measuring the amount of water displaced. (1 ml $= 1$cm^3)

SCIENCE, DESIGN & TECHNOLOGY:

What gives a brick wall stability? Investigate with different bond patterns of headers and sleepers, with double thickness walls, and with buttresses, using Lego building bricks.

Design, make and test a spirit level and a plumb line.

Devise a test to discover whether or not bricks absorb water.

Make a mould and construct some bricks. Use them for a small building project, e.g. sand-pit, barbecue, kiln, base for a bench.

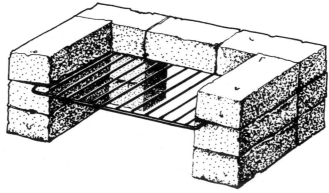

Experiment with different mortar mixes to find the most effective.

24

ART/CRAFT: Study brickwork patterns in walls and paths. Design tessellating patterns of bricks. One activity could be to design a wall using coloured bricks with your name built in.

Design a mural for a large brick wall.

Look carefully at and feel the surface texture of different types of brick.

Scratch the surface of a brick. Smell it. Look at it through a magnifying glass.

Brick-rubbings.

Sketch a brick.

COMPUTER PROGRAMS: *Brick up* (MEP Microprimer, Pack 3) (vocabulary exercises.)
Wall (SMILE The Next 17) (M.E.P.)
Various design or turtle graphics programs could be used for creating brick-shape tessellated patterns, e.g. *LOGO, DIAGRAMH,* etc.

MUSIC: *Follow the Yellow Brick Road* from *The Wizard of Oz,* J. Weinberger Ltd.
Goodbye Yellow Brick Road Elton John.
We're building a wall to surround Ourselves from *The Selfish Giant* cartoon film.

ENVIRONMENTAL STUDIES: Make a study of building materials through the ages.
Find out what bricks are made from and how they are made.
Study the effects of time and weather on brickwork.
Find out what you can about a bricklayer's job. How does he learn his trade? What tools does he use? How many bricks can he lay in a day?
Study local buildings. What materials are they made of? What types and colour of brick are used? Make a chart to illustrate your information.
Study the patterned brickwork of Tudor and Jacobean chimneys.
The work of a steeplejack.
How are bricks carried?
Find out about the brickwork in tunnels, bridges and viaducts.

P.E./GAMES: **Wall games: throwing and kicking skills. A variety of targets could be devised.**

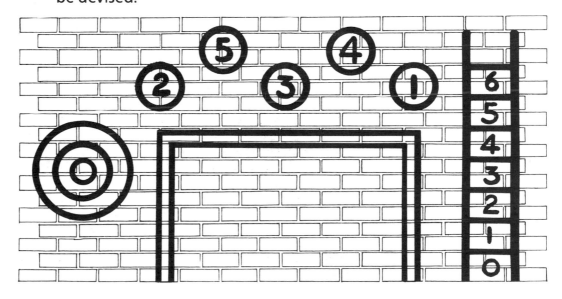

TOYS/GAMES:
Lego; various other plastic and wooden building bricks.
Design a game which can be played on a board laid out as a brick pattern.
Juggling with 3 wooden bricks. (The bricks are held at waist level and their surfaces kept horizontal.)
Design a Brick-Wall Maze:-

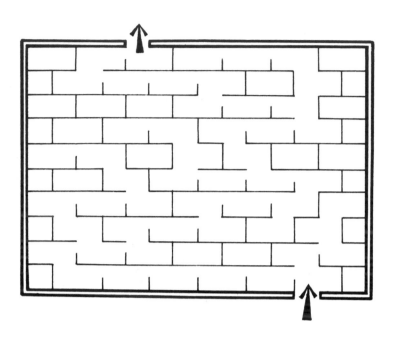

VISITS:
A local building site; a brickworks; Roman remains; Tudor and Jacobean buildings.

OTHER AREAS FOR DISCUSSION & INVESTIGATION:
Find out about: Header-Bond; Stretcher-Bond; English-Bond; Flemish-Bond.
How many bricks are there in a house? Estimate, calculate.
Use *The Guinness Book of Records* to discover:-
  (a) The greatest distance achieved for carrying a brick.
  (b) The largest number of bricks ever laid in one hour.
  (c) The record for brick lifting.
  (d) The greatest reported distance for throwing a brick.

clocks

DISCUSSION:

What would life be like without devices for telling the time?
What natural measures of time do we have? E.g. day and night, seasons, pulse.
When do we need to know the time?
What devices do we have for telling the time?
When do we need to measure periods of time?
3.15pm Tuesday, 5th January, 1988 A.D. Discuss the elements of this statement of time.
How time affects the lives of people in various occupations.

LANGUAGE:

Writing:
- A full-size time machine can be constructed in the classroom, and imaginative stories can be based on its use.
- *Lost in Time.* A machine enables the user to move freely backwards and forwards in time by setting a clock.
- *24 hours in the life of a clock.* A story told by the town square clock relating to different events happening around it as its *arms* change position.

Research:
Find out about: chronometer, grandfather clock, grandmother clock, Big Ben, lantern clock, carriage clock, dandelion clock, atomic clock, an horologist, chronology, digital and analogue watches, clepsydra.

27

Drama/Movement:
- Movement to the music of *The Clock Symphony*, by Haydn.
- Experiment with clockwork movements.
- Construct a Time Travel machine and act out various adventures.

Vocabulary:
Vocabulary associated with time and clock: punctual, delayed, schedule, timetable, timely, cog, dial, pendulum, clockwise, anti-clockwise, seldom, often, when, now, future, past, then, decade, century, etc.

Stories:
Peter Pan, James Barrie, Puffin.
'The Watch Dog' in The Phantom Toll Booth, Norton Juster, Collins.
The Time Machine, H. G. Wells, Dent.
The Clock Tower Ghost, Gene Kemp, Faber & Faber.

Poetry:
'Time Machine', Barbara Ireson, from *Rhyme Time 2*, Beaver Books.
'Days', Philip Larkin, from *Time's Delight* R. Wilson, Hamlyn.
Thirty Days has September. . . (Trad.)
'What does the clock say?' George Barker, in *Happenings 2*, Harrap.
'I used to have a little red alarm clock', Michael Rosen in *A Second Poetry Book*, OUP.
'The Watch', May Svenson in *Junior Voices, Book 4*, Penguin.
'Potato Clock', Roger McGough in *Sky in the Pie*, Puffin.

MATHEMATICS:

Planning operating times for automatic ovens — giving cooking instructions and times meals are required.

Telling the time to 1 hour; ½ and ¼ hours; 5 minutes; 1 minute; a.m. and p.m. times.

Fast and slow clocks; seconds, 24 hour clock; digital clocks and watches.

Showing times:
1. Time intervals.

START TIME **EAT MEAL ? MINUTES** **FINISH TIME**

2. Time trails

| Left home | Wait for bus 10 minutes | Bus journey 24 minutes | Walk to shop 7 minutes | Shopping 40 minutes |

Estimating and timing events – using stop watches, e.g. counting to 100, walking round the playground.

How a day is spent – Block graph or pie chart.

Timetables – planning journeys.

Estimating the time when the clock minute hand is missing.

Study of pendulums. Investigate different lengths with different weights attached, and different degrees of swing.

Clock Arithmetic (modulo arithmetic).

Fractions of an hour.

Use your calculator to discover how many seconds in a year.

SCIENCE, DESIGN & TECHNOLOGY:

Design and make a ten-second timer, as in illustration, or as helter-skelter in photograph.

Design an unusual clock face for a 'clock of the future'.

Investigate the efficiency of egg timers, alarm clocks.

Using cogs, design a simple clock face with an hour and minute hand. The 'Cogs' computer programme may be useful.

Design an experiment to investigate the cooling time of water.

Study the workings of an old clock.

Design and make a shadow clock or a candle clock.

Design and make a timer to time one minute/five minutes/one hour.

ART/CRAFT:

Collect cogs and pieces from old clocks and watches. Use them to design and make a collage.

Create designs and pictures using printing inks and clock pieces.

Design a child's *nursery* clock.

Sketch local clocks.

Experiment with clock face patterns.

COMPUTER PROGRAMS:

Time Trucker (ASK software from ESM)
Beat the Clock (Arnold Wheaton Software)
Timeman 1 and 2 (B.E.S)
Clocks (Mathematical Activities and Investigations) by Capital Media (ILECC)
Boileggs and *Clock* (Primary Maths. Northants C.E.C.)

MUSIC:
The Clock Symphony, Haydn.
'My Grandfather's Clock', *Popular Community Song Book*, No. 1, EMI Music.
'Hickory Dickory Dock', *Faber Book of Nursery Songs*, Faber.
Record some interesting clock chimes.
Compose an interesting chime for a clock for each quarter hour.
Study a metronome and find out why it is helpful to a musician.

ENVIRONMENTAL STUDIES:
Study the opening and closing times of local shops and services
Discover where in your local area you could find out the time if you did not have a watch. Mark these points on a local map.
Discuss the accuracy of the clocks you can see in the local area.
Investigate hours of daylight, the shortest day, the longest day.
Find out about the watch and clock industry in Switzerland.

P.E./GAMES:
Present a series of activities — e.g. skipping, running on the spot, throwing and catching a ball, stepping on and off a bench.
How many can each child achieve *against the clock*?
Compare children's times for athletic events with world records. (see Guinness Book of Records).
Compare pulse rates before and after exercise.
Play clock golf.
Clockwise and anti-clockwise movements.

TOYS AND GAMES:
Clock patience
Time Dominoes (E.J. Arnold)
Construction clock kits

VISITS:
A science museum
Big Ben
Astronomical Clock, e.g. Hampton Court Palace, Cathedrals.
Mechanical clocks on outsides of buildings (especially churches, cathedrals, shops, public buildings etc.)
Clocks and watches in jewellers' shops.

OTHER AREAS FOR DISCUSSION AND INVESTIGATION:
Estimating and passing of one minute (class competition).
Devices with automatic timers.
Greenwich Mean Time.
Time Zones.
International Date Line.
Roman Numerals on clocks.
Use *The Guinness Book of Records* to discover which is
    (a) the oldest surviving working clock
    (b) the largest clock in the world
    (c) the largest pendulum in the world
    (d) the most expensive clock
The derivation of the names of the days and the months.
The derivation of the word *clock* — French *Cloche*, German *Glocke* (from when monks recorded the passing of time by ringing the monastery bells).
Time on board ship.
Try to discover how to use your watch as a compass.

footwear

DISCUSSION:

Do we really need shoes?
The purpose of different types of footwear.
The importance of properly fitting shoes.
Looking after boots and shoes.

LANGUAGE:

Writing:
- Write about what it would be like if one of the following came into your possession:
  1) Seven league boots
  2) Mercury's talaria (winged sandals)
- *Bare-footed.* Write about life without shoes.
- You have bought a pair of expensive shoes. When you put them on to go to an important party you find the shop assistant has packed two shoes of different sizes. Write a letter of complaint to the manager of the shop.

Research:
Find out as much as you can about: bootee, boot hook, bootikin, boot-jack, bootlegger, blucher, brogue, buskin, clog, court shoes, flip-flops, flippers, foot muff, galoshes, jack-boot, moccasin, mule, platform shoes, plimsoll, roller boots, running spikes, sabot, sandal, shoe-horn, shoeing-smith, shoe-rose, shoeshine boy, shoestring, shoetree, slipper, snow-shoes, stiletto heel, tap-shoes, trainers, wellington boot, winkle-pickers.

Drama/Movement:

- A conversation between two shoes about their owner, and the way they are treated.
- The Invisible Man. A drama with various characters including an invisible person represented by a pair of clogs, which are moved across the floor by means of pieces of string attached to the soles.
- Walk around the hall miming the effects of wearing different types of footwear e.g. divers' boots, ballet shoes, skis.

Vocabulary:

Parts of a shoe – upper; toecap; vamp; tongue; quarter sole; welt; insole; heel; patten; lace; buckle; strap; eyelet.
Cobbler; shod; last; instep.

Phrases and Sayings:

Given the boot; on a shoe string; boot licker; step into someone else's shoes; the boot is on the other foot; to have one's heart in one's boots; to shake in one's shoes; a cobbler should stick to his last; cobbler's children worst shod.

Stories:

Alfie's Feet, Shirley Hughes, The Bodley Head.
The Elves and the Shoemaker, Ladybird Books.
Seven League Boots, Puffin.
Cinderella (Trad).
Boots of the Holly Tree Inn, Charles Dickens, Penguin.
'The New Boots' by Grace Foakes, in *The Green Story House,* Oxford University Press.

Poetry:

'The Hobnail Boots What Farver Wore' (trad English) in *Junior Voices Book 4,* Penguin.
'If You Don't Put Your Shoes On' by Michael Rosen in *A Second Poetry Book,* Oxford University Press.
'The Thinker' by William Carlos Williams in *Junior Voices Book 2,* Penguin.
'The Lost Shoe', Walter de la Mare in *Poems,* Puffin.
'A Pair of Slippers' by E. V. Rieu in *A Puffin quartet of Poets,* Penguin.

MATHEMATICS:

Whose shoes cover the largest area? Draw the outline of each person's shoe on centimetre squared paper, and calculate the areas covered.

Investigate shoe sizes and how these are measured in different countries.

Draw a graph to illustrate the different shoe sizes in the class.

How many shoes might be worn at any one time by the people in (a) the class (b) the school (c) your village or town (d) the country.

Measure the weights of (a) shoes worn by children in the class (b) different types of boots and shoes. Draw a graph to show the results.

Consider the costs of different shoes. Does the cost of shoes depend on the size?

Measure the dimensions of feet in your class (a) length (b) width. Draw a graph to illustrate your findings.

A shopkeeper can afford to stock only 100 pairs of children's shoes. How many of each size should he stock. Investigate.

SCIENCE, DESIGN & TECHNOLOGY:

Who would find the following useful — rubber-soled shoes, magnetic boots, weighted boots?

Make a collection of different sorts of boots and shoes. Investigate what type of sole is most suitable for: (a) a slippery surface (b) a wet surface, (c) a firm grip on grass (d) playing football in the playground.

Construct a storage system which will hold 6 pairs of shoes, and which takes up as little space as possible.

Design a device to make easier the job of polishing shoes.

Make a shoe scraper and cleaner for cleaning muddy shoes.

A comparison of different materials used for making shoes. Devise tests for durability, adhesion, flexibility, etc.

Design and make an instrument for measuring foot sizes.

ART/CRAFT:

Design and draw a pair of shoes which you would like to wear to a party.

Paint a picture based on (a) The Old Woman Who Lived in a Shoe
                    (b) Puss in Boots
                    (c) Cinderella's Glass Slipper
                    (d) Clementine's Herring Box Sandals

Make a pair of moccasins.

Patterns with foot prints and sole prints.

Invent and draw a pair of special shoes for 1. James Bond (007). 2. A robot. 3. A fisherman.

Use a shoe box to make (a) a diorama (b) a weaving loom (c) a musical instrument.

Decorate an old pair of shoes using oil paints.

What can you make from an old shoe? E.g. Garden, pencil holder, monster etc.

MUSIC:	'Clementine', *Appuskidu*, A. & C. Black.
ENVIRONMENTAL STUDIES:	Study the different footwear people require because of the jobs they do. The story of a leather shoe from hide to foot. How are shoes repaired? Footwear in other countries. Find out how a blacksmith shoes a horse. The history of footwear. Study the different types of shoe fastenings. St. Crispin is the patron saint of shoemakers. Find out what you can about him.
P.E./GAMES:	Investigate the different types of sports shoes. Make a collection of the various studs and attachments that are fitted to the soles of these shoes, and explain their uses. Novelty races wearing adult size shoes. A detection game – Footprints can be made in a sandpit. By studying the footprints, try to work out what the person was doing (e.g. running, hopping, carrying a heavy load, etc.) and also try to identify the person by studying the shoes of a group of children. Roller skating, ice skating and skate boarding.
VISITS:	Shoe factory. Shoe repairer. Shoe shop. A Tannery.
OTHER AREAS FOR DISCUSSION AND INVESTIGATION:	Use *The Guinness Book of Records* to discover:- (a) the most expensive shoes that can be purchased. (b) the largest shoes ever sold. (c) the record for the number of shoes cleaned in 8 hours. Investigate shoe lacing patterns (lacing cards can be used). Why do Muslims leave their shoes at the door before entering a mosque? Find out about:- Boot Hill Cemetery; the hotel servant called 'Boots'; fashion footwear. Investigate the following old superstitions: (a) a horseshoe is a good luck emblem (b) a shoe tied behind a honeymoon couple's car brings good luck (c) it is unlucky to put on the left shoe before the right or either shoe on the wrong foot.

1520   1600   1650   1720   1830   1905   1930   1950   1980

hats and headgear

DISCUSSION: Different types of hats and headgear and their purpose.
Hats associated with famous people (e.g. Sherlock Holmes, Charlie Chaplin, Tommy Cooper, Davy Crockett, Punch, Frank Spencer, Noddy, Lawrence of Arabia).

LANGUAGE:

Writing:
- *The hat which makes you invisible.*
- Write a limerick or poem about someone who wears an unusual hat.
- Write an article as the fashion editor for a class magazine reviewing hats you have made or collected. Include design sketches.

Research:
There are many names for different kinds of headgear. Find out about: bath-, bobble-, bowler-, cardinal's-, chimney-pot-, cloche-, cocked-, coolie-, cowboy-, dunce's-, jester's-, opera-, panama-, porkpie-, straw-, ten gallon-, top-, tricorn-HAT; black-, forage-, mob-, night-, skull-CAP; bowler, burnous, busby, bush-hat, cap and bells, coronet, cowl, crash helmet, crown, deer-stalker, fedora, fez, head-dress, Homburg, hood, stetson, tiara, tam o'shanter, trilby, topper, toupee, turban, wimple, earmuffs, eye-shade, headband, kerchief, mask, visor, wig.

Drama/Movement:
- Devise a drama in which the characters are identified only by their headgear.
- Study of headgear in theatre costume.

Vocabulary

Brim, chinstrap, cloth, doff, don, felt, hatband, hat-box, hatful, hat-less, hatpeg, hatpin, hat-stand, hatter, mask, milliner, muslin, peak, periwig, size, veil, wig.

Phrases and Sayings:

Hat trick, to hang one's hat, to pass round the hat, to take one's hat off to, to talk through one's hat, mad as a hatter, my hat!, to keep it under your hat, at the drop of a hat, to eat one's hat, cap in hand, a feather in one's cap, if the cap fits wear it, to put on your thinking cap, knocked into a cocked hat, to be 'capped' for your club, county or country.

Stories:

'The Mad Hatter' in *Alice in Wonderland*, Lewis Carroll, Collins Classics.
The Silver Crown R. O. Brien, Collins Lions.

Poetry:

'My Hat', Stevie Smith in *My Kind of Verse,* Burke Books.
'The Quangle Wangle's Hat', Edward Lear, *Once Upon a Rhyme,* Faber and Faber.
'Mart was my best friend', Michael Rosen, from *You Tell Me,* Puffin Books.
'The Old Person of Fratton', Limerick from *Let's Read Some Poetry,* Allman & Sons.

MATHEMATICS:

Find out how hat sizes are measured.

Devise a method for measuring head sizes (circumference and diameters) for the purpose of hat-fitting. Use your method to measure head sizes of children in the class or school. Record your results on a graph. How does head size vary with age?

How popular is the wearing of hats? Carry out a survey in your local High Street at a busy time. List and classify the types of headgear.

Consider the overall percentage of hat wearers, the most popular type of hat, and the most popular material and colour.

Hats are frequently packaged in cylindrical or cuboid containers. Work out the dimensions of the most appropriate containers for a range of different hats.

Hat Mix-ups: 3 people leaving a party each take the wrong hat. In how many different ways can three hats be mixed up? In how many ways can 4, 5, 6 hats be mixed?

Work out the length of ribbon which would be required to make a headband for every child in the class.

Make a top hat (flat oval brim and cylindrical body) from card to fit a friend's head. Begin with accurate head measurements. Work out the surface area of the hat.

HAT-TRICK PUZZLE:
Find the values of the different kinds of hat in this addition table.
Then find the missing total.
Make up some similar hat addition tables using your own hat designs.

				32
				40
				60
38	40	60	**188**

SCIENCE, DESIGN & TECHNOLOGY:

Design an unusual but effective hat stand.

Invent a 'magic' trick for which a top-hat is necessary.

Design and make a hat which also has another use – e.g. as a purse, insect repellent, tea-cosy.

Design a hat which will give shelter from sun and rain as well as providing a cooling system for hot weather and a heater for cold weather.

ART/CRAFT:

Organise a class or school 'Easter Parade' with hats designed and made by the children. Utilise some of the following for decoration – bows, flowers, ribbon, sequins, feathers, beads, frills, diamanté, coloured netting, glitter, shells, pasta, pom-poms, braiding, silver, gold and coloured foil, tissue and crepe paper.

Make a collage with pictures of hats and headgear cut out from magazines, newspapers and periodicals.

Make a tie-dye kerchief.

Use a balloon as a base for making a papier mâché space-, crash-, Roman, Viking or other helmet.

Design and draw, paint or make:-
1. An elaborate crown for a king or queen;
2. A novelty hat with a motif which has a message;
3. A 'Runcible Hat' (as in Edward Lear's 'Courtship of the Yonghy-Bonghy-Bò').
4. Hats for 'living' chess pieces.

37

| **MUSIC:** | 'Where Did you Get That Hat?' in *The Jolly Herring*, A. & C. Black.
'All Around My Hat', Traditional Folk Song.
'In Your Easter Bonnet', *Appuskidu*, A. & C. Black.
'The Three-Cornered Hat', De Falla.
'Mexican Hat Dance', *Dancing Games for all Ages*, E. Nelson, Sterling Publ. |

ENVIRONMENTAL STUDIES.

Study of headgear in other countries.
Study of headgear at different periods in history.
Make a class collection of as many types of hat and headgear as possible. Find photographs or drawings of those you are not able to collect.
From what materials are hats made? Where do the raw materials come from? What can you find out about a milliner's trade?
Investigate — hats for different seasons and different weather conditions.
— hats and headgear as used for sports, e.g. skiing, boxing, riding, motoring.
— headgear worn for religious purposes.
— headgear worn for polar exploration and in the desert.
— hats worn as part of a uniform.
— hats denoting rank or position.
— fashion in hats: hats as ornament ('Ascot' hats).
Find out about the Tudor Cap in architecture. Look for this in buildings of the Tudor and Stuart periods.

TOYS/GAMES:

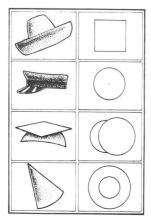

Who can make the best hat from one sheet of newspaper?
Design and make a matching game with cut-outs of hats and people.
Can you find an item of headgear beginning with each letter of the alphabet?
Throwing balls into hats: knocking hats off model heads: hat-juggling: rabbit-in-a-hat tricks: Musical Hats.
There are many parlour games which involve 'capping' verses, names, words, proverbs, sentences. Each player has to continue the sequence by starting with the last letter used.

Hat-matching: Connect the different perspective views of the same hat.

VISITS:

Museums — fashion and social history sections.
Fashion warehouse; large department store;
commercial art college design department; milliner's shop.
An Easter Bonnet parade.

OTHER AREAS FOR DISCUSSION AND INVESTIGATION:

Use *The Guinness Book of Records* to find —
(a) the highest price ever paid for a hat.
(b) which cricketer has achieved the greatest number of hat-tricks.
Make full-size drawings/paintings of different types of headgear.
Cut them out and display them on a wall frieze with associated pictures and descriptive and imaginative writing in prose and verse.
How many badges can you fit onto a hat?
Why is a hat-trick so called?

ladders

DISCUSSION: Why do we use ladders?
Who needs ladders, and for what purpose?
Are ladders always used for climbing?
Possible dangers when using a ladder.

LANGUAGE:

Writing:
- An escape story involving the use of a ladder.
- The work of a steeplejack. Try to imagine his feelings.
- *Walking under a ladder brings bad luck.* Write a story suggesting how this superstition might have arisen.
- Write a story based on a photograph or picture showing a ladder in use.
- Explain the operation of an extension ladder.

Research:
Find out about —
Ladder-back chair; ladder stitch; scaling ladder; companion ladder; Jacob's ladder; siege ladder; fish ladder; turntable ladder; extension ladder.

39

Drama/Movement:
Mime: Climbing different types of ladders; rescue by ladder; storming a castle.

Vocabulary:
rung, extend, extension, ascent, upright, incline, angle, climb, descent.

Word ladders:

gigantic	eight
huge	seven
large	six
big	five
medium	four
small	three
tiny	two
minute	one

Word staircases:

```
cat                    boat
  i                       r
  new                     e
    e                     exit
    top                      a
      o                      i
      dog                    lost
        u                       a
        nut                     l
                                loot
```

Acrostics. . .based on *ladder*.
Making words from the letters of the word 'ladder'.

MATHEMATICS:
Ordinal number and place value: placing numbers in order on a ladder.
c.f. Computer program *Boxes* (Microsmile 1 M.E.P.) This can also be played with a set of numbered blocks and ladders with a selected number of spaces.
Draw a ladder at various angles of incline to a wall. Investigate the angles in a triangle. Investigate the ladder height in relation to the angle of incline.
Determine the length of wood required to produce the (a) rungs (b) uprights, for a particular ladder.
Parallel lines.
Scale drawings of ladders.

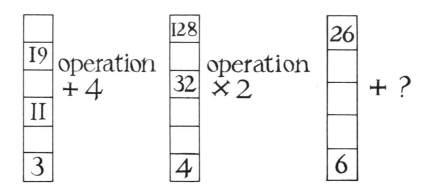

The same operation is repeated to produce the numbers in successive spaces. Work out the operation in the third example. Calculators will be helpful.

SCIENCE, DESIGN & TECHNOLOGY:
Investigate the different angles of incline of a ladder with reference to safety.
Investigate the materials used for making ladders, list their properties and problems. (E.g. Is a wooden ladder preferable to a metal ladder on a cold day?)
Given a limited supply of materials, (e.g. balsa wood, string, card, matchsticks) design and make a ladder to serve a particular purpose.
Find out about the Jacob's ladder plant.
Design and make a model of a siege ladder, giving protection to invading soldiers.
Design and make a miniature rope ladder investigating a variety of knots.
Design an item to prevent a ladder slipping on a particular surface.
Design a set of steps to stand on a staircase.
Design a safety feature for a ladder.
Design and construct a model of a piece of playground apparatus which incorporates ladders.

ART/CRAFT:
Draw a ladder from different perspectives.
Design and draw an advertisement for selling a ladder.
Incorporate a ladder motif in pattern making; card edge printing or stencil.

COMPUTER PROGRAMS:
Diagramh (Design program Newman College).
Describe how, in *Magic Adventure*, a ladder helps to find the way to the castle. (Northants C.E.C.)

MUSIC:
Work on *musical ladders* (scales).
Compose a piece of music entitled "The Ladder" conveying the feeling of ascending, descending, slipping, etc.
Song: 'We are climbing Jacob's ladder'. (Youth Praise Bk. 2. Falcon).

ENVIRONMENTAL STUDIES:
Siege ladders.
The development of ladders.
A study of ladders on telegraph poles. Count the numbers of rungs on the ladders. Note the pattern and placement of rungs. Are they the same on all poles? Why are they there? Why don't they start at ground

level?
The Fire Service
Pot Holing.
Ascents. Various ascents in the country called Jacob's ladder.
Ladder Hills in Scotland.
Salmon Ladders. (e.g. In relation to the Scottish hydro-electric project).
Locks on canals.

P.E./GAMES

Using rope ladders, P.E. ladder.
Using wall bars.
Chinese ladders: Children lie flat with feet facing their partner. Each pair is given a number. When a number is called the two children with that number jump up, run over the rungs (children's legs) of the ladder, back along the sides of the ladder and then over the rungs until they return to their original place. The first child to return gains a point for the team.

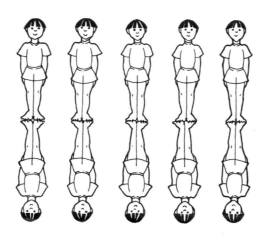

Competition ladders. (e.g. chess ladder).

TOYS/GAMES:

Snakes and ladders.
Design and make a game incorporating ladders.

VISITS:

Local Fire Station.
Street Lighting Department.
Building Site.
Windmill.
Gasometer.

OTHER AREAS FOR DISCUSSION & INVESTIGATION:

Study a range of other items used for climbing and descending. (Window cleaner's cradle, stiles, ramps, scaffolding, etc.)
Use *The Guinness Book of Records* to discover the longest ladder in the U.K./World.
Investigate the length of other ladders. (Fireman's; gerbil's etc.).
Compare the lengths of other ladders with your P.E. ladder.
Investigate superstitions. (Walking under a ladder is considered to be the most commonly held superstition).
Discuss how two ladders each 4 metres long might be used to cross a crevasse 6 metres wide.

letters

DISCUSSION:
Why do people write letters now that we have the telephone?
Consider which different methods have been used for sending messages.
For what different purposes are letters sent?
What factors need to be considered when letter boxes are fitted?
If a large number of copies of one letter are to be distributed, how can modern technology help?

LANGUAGE:

Writing:
- Study the start, finish and layout of different types of correspondence, e.g. business letters, personal letters, postcards.
- Practise a clear method of addressing envelopes.
- Write an interesting *Thank You* letter.
- Write to an author giving your views on a book you have recently read.
- Write a letter of complaint to a T.V. company about a programme you did not like.
- Write a report of a school event and send it to a local newspaper.
- Write a letter which could have been written by:-
    1. a castaway sending a message in a bottle
    2. a hostage
    3. a dissatisfied customer
    4. a spy
    5. an explorer.

Research:
Find out about:- air mail, commemorative and definitive stamps, an epistle, letter-cards, letters patent, letterhead, cartology, deltiology, recorded delivery, C.O.D., registered post, certificate of posting, re-directed mail, love-letters, mail order, mail train, mail bag, mail boat, mail coach, mail van, pigeon post, writing case, seal, franking machine, s.a.e,

43

philately, phosphorous bands, post-code.

Drama/Movement:
Mime different reactions to the receipt of a letter.
Pass on the news to a second person, still in mime. Can the audience guess the contents of the letter?

Vocabulary:
address, communication, correspondence, envelope, faithfully, flap, frank, letter-box, message, philatelist, pillar box, postage, postal, postmark, sincerely, stationery.

Stories:
King Rollo's Letter and Other Stories, David McKee, Andersen Press.
The Epistles of the New Testament;
'The Man Who Pinched God's Letter' in *The Faithless Lollybird* by Joan Aiken, Jonathan Cape.

Poetry:
'How to Write a Letter' by Elizabeth Turner (1775–1846) in *Oxford Book of Children's Verse*, OUP.
'Night Mail' by W. H. Auden in *Oxford Book of Verse for Juniors: Book 3*, OUP.
'Posting Letters' by Gregory Harrison in *Happenings 2*, Harrap.
'The Postman' by Jon Stallworthy in *Poems and Pictures – Town and Country*, Evans.
'This Letter's to Say' by Raymond Wilson in *A Fourth Poetry Book*, OUP.

MATHEMATICS:

A study of the cost of sending letters by airmail to different countries.

Work out the costs of delivering letters and/or parcels of different weights in this country and to other countries. Use scales for practical activities wherever possible.

Find out the area of paper required to make a standard-size letter-writing pad.

Draw nets which could be used to make envelopes of given dimensions.

Use the scale in an atlas to work out how far letters have travelled.

In a book of stamps costing £1 and containing no more than 10 stamps, which stamps would it be best to include?

How far would you have to walk from your home or school to buy a stamp at your nearest post office?

Keep a record of how many letters are received at home and/or school each day for a month. Calculate totals and averages per day. Show your results on a graph.

Post a letter to a classmate. How many hours does it take before the letter is received? Make comparison with letters sent and received by others.

Use a current stamp catalogue to find out the value of mint and used stamps. How do these compare with the stamp's face value?

SCIENCE, DESIGN & TECHNOLOGY:

Design and make a model of a pillar-box of the future.

Design and make a new style of envelope.

Make a decorative, but practical, letter-opener.

Incorporate a piece of sponge in a device which dampens the gum in order to seal envelopes.

Design a special bicycle for a postman.

Investigate the writing of letters in invisible ink.
Draw diagrams and a plan of a Post Office of the future, giving consideration to security, and to providing an efficient service for customers.

DONT WASTE A SECOND, COME JUST AS YOU ARE

WE LONG TO HEAR THE CLATTER OF YOUR LITTLE FEET

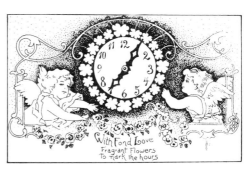

With Fond Loove
Fragrant Flowers
To mark the hours

ART/CRAFT:

Investigate and experiment with different styles of handwriting.

Make a letter-rack.

Create a personalised design for decorating matching letter-paper and envelopes.

Design postage stamps and a distinctive postmark for your town or school.

Design a comfortable and practical uniform for a postman and a postwoman.

COMPUTER PROGRAMS:

Word-Processing software (see notes on use of computers in project studies)
Electronic Mail facility – as available on The Times Network System (TTNS) and PRESTEL.
Puzzle Farm (M.E.P. *Infant and First Schools* Disc)
Off-Line Letter Writer (Derbyshire Educational Software Centre)

MUSIC:

'I sent a letter to my love', Trad.

ENVIRONMENTAL STUDIES:

Find out how the postal service operates. How does a letter reach its destination after it has been posted?
Make a collection of different stamps from around the world. Find the countries of origin on a globe and in an atlas.

Make a collection of different postmarks from letters posted within your own country. Locate the places of origin on a map.

What are your local postcodes? Study the national system of postcodes.

Study the history of sending letters and the postal service.

Investigate the making of paper and how watermarks are made.

Find out where letters can be posted in your area. Mark these points on a map. Make a study of different local pillar-boxes. What information on each is given about collection times?

Famous letters in history.

What can you buy at a post office besides stamps? Investigate.

Collect postcards showing different places. What can you find out about the different locations from the pictures on the cards?

What is the standard map sign for a post office? How many post offices can you find on a map of your area?

Look for the correspondence columns in your local newspaper.

What issues are currently being discussed? What are your views? Can you find out from your local library what was being discussed 25 or 50 years ago?

VISITS:

Local Post Office.

Invite someone connected with the local postal service to talk about their job.

The Philatelic Counter at a large Post Office.

OTHER AREAS FOR DISCUSSION & INVESTIGATION:

Use *The Guinness Book of Records* to discover:-

    (a) The longest letter ever written;

    (b) The shortest letter ever written;

    (c) The most letters ever received by one person in a year;

    (d) The longest time recorded for correspondence between pen-pals.

Find out how far your local postman walks in a day. How far will he walk in a year? . . . in his working life?

Find out about the magazines which are available for stamp and postcard collectors.

Find out about letters requesting money and gifts — such as those from Charities, and begging letters.

Find out about:

the Universal Postal Union.

the Postmaster-General.

Rowland Hill and the Penny Post.

postage due stamps.

Wells Fargo.

chain letters.

unsolicited mail.

graphology (telling character and fortunes through a study of handwriting).

People sometimes write letters in code. Work out and send a coded message of your own.

Try to make contact with another school to initiate pen-pal correspondence.

Study forms of address when writing letters. How would you begin a letter to, e.g. the Prime Minister, your Member of Parliament, a bishop, the Queen, a lord, a doctor?

mirrors

DISCUSSION:
Different types of mirror and their uses (e.g. rear view, concealed entrance, make-up mirrors).
Why do restaurants sometimes have large mirrors on one of the walls?
Why do dentists need to use a mirror?
The Daily Mirror. Do you think this is a good title for a newspaper?
What did people use before mirrors were invented?
Consider different surfaces that reflect.
The word 'AMBULANCE' is sometimes written on vehicles in mirror writing. Why is this?

LANGUAGE:

Writing:
- Look in a mirror and then write a description of your face so that your classmates might recognise you from your account.
- Write a story about what happens when one of the following mirrors comes into your possession.
1. *Merlin's Magic Mirror* which informed King Ryence of treason, secret plots and planned invasions:
2. *Vulcan's Mirror* which showed the past, present and future.
3. *Reynard's Wonderful Mirror* which showed what was happening one mile away.

Research:
Find out what you can about: mirror images, mirror machine, cheval-glass, speculum, helioscope, heliograph, praxinoscope, heliostat, camera obscura, siderostat, coelostat, reflecting telescope, reflecting microscope, concave-, convex-, distorting-, rotating-, plane-, parabolic-mirrors, mirror paper.

Drama/Movement:
- Children work in pairs, facing each other. One child is the object while the other child is the mirror image which reflects each movement.
- Act the story of *Echo and Narcissus* or that of *The Lady of Shalott* from the Arthurian Romances.
- The story of Snow White (Mirror, mirror on the wall).

47

Vocabulary:
Concave, convex, decorated, distortion, frame, glass, image, looking glass, plane, reflection, shatter, silvering, surface, symmetry.

Stories:
'How the Polar Bear Became' in *How the Whale Became & Other Stories* by Ted Hughes, Young Puffin.
'The Squire's Tale', from Chaucer's *Canterbury Tales* (Modern Translation by Nevill Coghill, Penguin).
The Dog and its Shadow, Aesop's Fables, Penguin.
Alice Through the Looking Glass by Lewis Carroll, Penguin.
Echo and Narcissus, Greek Myth.
'Mirror, Mirror', in *Garfield's Apprentices*, Leon Garfield, Piccolo Pan Books.

Poetry:
'Mirror, Mirror' by Robert Graves in *Thoughtshapes*, OUP.
'The Lady of Shalott' by Alfred Lord Tennyson (suggested version illustrated by Charles Keeping), OUP.

MATHEMATICS:

Use plane mirrors to investigate symmetrical shapes.

Draw half shapes so that, when a mirror is placed on one edge, a complete shape appears. Which letters of the alphabet can be produced in this way?

Which numbers up to 100 are symmetrical?

Use a mirror to investigate the number of lines of symmetry in regular polygons.

Investigate angles of incidence and angles of reflection.

Plot mirror images of given shapes on squared paper and use a mirror to check the results.

How many mirror tiles, each measuring 15cm × 15cm, would be required to construct a large mirror (a) of given surface area? (b) of given dimensions?

SCIENCE, DESIGN & TECHNOLOGY:

Make a cylinder from mirror paper. Draw designs on a sheet of paper which reflect as recognisable shapes in the cylindrical mirror.

Using mirror paper, try to construct some miniature distorting mirrors.

Construct a kaleidoscope using 2 rectangular mirrors and a piece of blank card of the same size held together to make a triangular prism. Tiny beads, sequins and coloured paper shapes placed in a transparent cellophane envelope at one end can be used to complete the kaleidoscope.

Investigate repetitive images by placing two plane mirrors in parallel.

Use mirrors and boxes or tubes of card to construct a periscope.

Experiment with methods of reflecting a light source to send messages by Morse Code.

Devise a system of mirrors which enables you to view the back of your head

Study lateral inversions as produced in mirror images.

Use mirrors in the design and production of a piece of equipment for looking round corners.

Investigate the distortions caused by (a) concave, (b) convex mirrors. Study the reflections in a large shiny dessert spoon.

Make a spectrograph to break up the sun's light into its constituent colours (spectrum): Place a plate or dish on a window-sill. Pour in water to a depth of about 1.5cm. Stand a small mirror in the water at an angle and the light will be reflected from the mirror in colour bands of the spectrum onto a wall or onto a piece of card held facing the mirror. Investigate objects as reflected in 2 mirrors taped together along one edge. Note the changes in reflection as the angle between the mirrors is altered. Try adjusting the mirrors until you can see half of your own face in each.

ART/CRAFT:

Draw your face as you imagine it to be. Look in a mirror and draw a self-portrait. What differences do you notice between your two pictures?

Design an unusual mirror frame.
Look carefully at the pattern formed in a kaleidoscope. Create kaleidoscope patterns using colouring pens, coloured gummed shapes or paint.

Create symmetrical *mirror* patterns based on the folding of paper immediately after applying ink or paint. Make a bookmark or a book cover design in this way.

Look for mirrors which have pictures or designs painted or inscribed on them. Experiment with painting on old mirrors.

Create posters, labels, signs, book titles, etc. using horizontal and/or vertical mirror-writing.

COMPUTER PROGRAMS:

Symmetry (MEP Microprimer Pack No. 4.)
Snooker for the investigation of angles of incidence and reflection on *SMILE – The 1st 31* MEP-Capital Region.

ENVIRONMENTAL STUDIES:
Find out how mirrors are made.
Make a collection of drawings and photographs of as many different mirrors as possible.
How many mirrors do you have in your home? Collect and record information about their purpose, position, dimension.
How do shopkeepers make use of mirrors?
Investigate the use of mirrors by customers in clothes and shoe shops.
Investigate the use of internal and external mirrors on a car or van.
Try positioning mirrors in a stationary car to achieve the best results i.e. the smallest 'blind' area.
Find out how holograms are created and used.
How does the moon act as a mirror?

TOYS/GAMES:
In which sports do mirrors play a part?
Obtain a long mirror and use it to produce amusing reflections.

Try to knock over targets by first bouncing a ball off a wall.
Children view through a mirror a message written on a black/white board. Who is the first to read it?
Kaleidoscope; Periscope; Praxinoscope.

VISITS:
The Hall of Mirrors at a Fun Fair.
Laser Shows.

OTHER AREAS FOR DISCUSSION AND INVESTIGATION:
Discuss the superstition that to break a mirror brings bad luck.
What are the suggested antidotes?
Use *The Guinness Book of Records* to find the weight of the mirror in the world's largest reflecting telescope.
Discover how to make it look as though a mirror is cracked by drawing lines on it with soap.
What were the properties of Alasnam's Mirror in the Arabian Nights story?
The Mirror of Diana is the name of a lake in the Alban Hills in Italy. Investigate reflections in water and make a collection of related pictures.
Find out about the Hall of Mirrors in the Palace of Versailles.

money

DISCUSSION:

Why is money necessary?

Money is the root of all evil . . . . Discuss the different effects that money can have on people.

Security — how can we look after our money?

Money management.

Which people deal with money in their jobs?

Will coins and notes eventually disappear?

What is the difference between the intrinsic value and the nominal value of a coin.

What is meant by the term millionaire?

LANGUAGE:

Writing:
- You have been left a fortune. Explain how this will affect your life, and write about your plans for the future.
- *How I became a millionaire.*

Research:
Find out as much as you can about: Money-changer; money-grubber; money order; milled edge; circumscription; exergue; money spider; exchange rates; coin of the realm; pin-money; lump sum; numismatics; I.O.U.; credit card; postal order; legal tender; penny dreadful.

Drama/Movement:
- Children dress up as different coins and argue their superiority based on size, value, usefulness, colour, etc.
- The Market Place. Scenes of buying and selling, bartering, indecision, pressure selling, etc.
- Act out the *Pardoner's Tale* — Chaucer.

51

Vocabulary:
Moneyed; coinage, obverse; reverse; value; cheque; deposit; withdraw; income; expenditure; counterfeit; mint; tokens; credit; debit; thrift; spendthrift; miser; currency; money's-worth; borrow; lend; capital; remittance; solvent; vault; barter; cash; till; cashier; account; receipt; invoices; numismatist; bankrupt; forgery; discount; impecunious.

Phrases and Sayings:
In mint condition; money spinner; for my money; to make money; put your money where you mouth is; in the money; in the red; money for old rope; money talks; in for a penny in for a pound; penny wise, pound foolish; penny pinching; on the toss of a coin; pocket money; ready money; penny for your thoughts; worth a pretty penny; look after the pennies and the pounds will take care of themselves; blank cheque.

Stories:
A Hundred Million Francs, Paul Berna, Puffin.
A Christmas Carol, Charles Dickens, Puffin Classics.
'The Widow's Mite', and many other stories from the Bible.
'The Pardoner's Tale' Chaucer's *Canterbury Tales,* Penguin.

Poetry:
'Hot Cross Buns'. Trad.
'Money Moans' by Roger McGough in *Sky in the Pie*, Puffin.
'He was a strong but simple man' by Gregory Harrison in *A Fourth Poetry Book,* Oxford University Press.
'Pocket Money' by Mick Gowar in *A Fifth Poetry Book,* O.U.P.
'The Penny Fiddle' by Robert Graves in *Junior Voices Book 1,* Penguin.

MATHEMATICS:

The following can be investigated in relation to a study of money: Shopping, discounts, percentages, exchange rates, foreign currency, a school bank, probability, pocket money, bills, receipts.

Consider the purchasing power of the coins and notes in circulation.

Study the costs of expensive items, e.g. car, house, jewellery.

Investigate the relationships between the values and weights of coins.

Shopping activities, especially the method employed for giving change, and the value of estimating.

Writing menus and working out bills (use of calculator).

Estimate the number of heads and tails in 100 spins – investigate.

Investigate the combinations of heads and tails when 2, 3 or 4 coins are spun. Carry out trials and draw graphs of the results.

Measure the diameters, widths and circumferences of circular coins as accurately as possible.

SCIENCE, DESIGN & TECHNOLOGY:

Design and make a holder for carrying coins.

Make an interesting box for a charity collection in which the coins embark on an elaborate journey before entering the box.

Devise a method for carrying bank notes safely.

Design and construct a device which will flip or roll a coin so that it will always show tails when it comes to rest.

Design and construct a game for a school fair which involves rolling coins down a wooden channel.

Design and make a device for sorting coins.

Examine coins through a magnifying glass.

Investigate for different coin patterns, c.f. Newton's cradle.

Try to study the workings of a coin operated machine.

ART/CRAFT: Design and draw the obverse and reverse of coins which display the heads of children and appropriate individual shields.

Coin rubbings: embossing using card or silver foil or with a pencil.

Make a *piggy bank* for a young child using papier mâché: snout – bottom of paper cup; legs – toilet roll; tail – pipe cleaner. Sticky-tape snout and legs on before papier mâché.

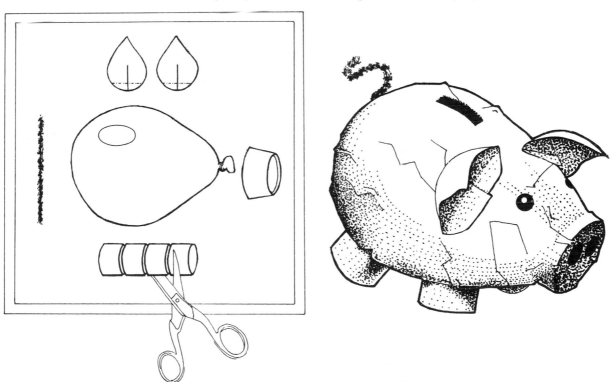

Make a purse or wallet.
Design a new set of coins and bank notes for your country – include all the features of coins and notes in circulation.

COMPUTER PROGRAMS: *Shopping* (M.E.P. Microprimer Pack I)
Coins (E.A.R.O. Software)
Taxi (Microsmile 2 – The Next 17 M.E.P.)
Money Plus (Fernleaf.)

MUSIC:	'Magic Penny' in *Alleluya*, A. & C. Black.
ENVIRONMENTAL STUDIES:	The mint — history and present day operation. Investigate the workings of a bank, including the services offered. A study of old coins and notes. Investigate precautions taken to prevent counterfeiting or defacing coins. Study of foreign money. Find out about the metals used for different coins. Study and name the currencies of other countries. Try to find coins that are not circular. A study of bank cheques and bank cards and how the systems work. Bank cash machines — how do they produce the correct amount of money on request? A study of how money is transferred from place to place. Security vans, etc.
TOYS/GAMES:	Money dominoes.

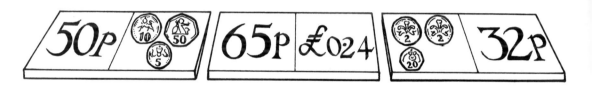

Monopoly.
Catching coins placed in a pile on your elbow. How many can you catch?
Shove-halfpenny.
Coin football.
Make a collection of coin games and conjuring tricks.

VISITS:	A bank worker could visit the school. Museums. Archaeological sites. A speaker from a local numismatic society could visit.
OTHER AREAS FOR DISCUSSION AND INVESTIGATION:	Why are some foreign coins made with holes in the centre? Bank money scales. Collect and study some coin magazines. The numbers on bank notes. *Heads I win. . .tails you lose!* Consider.

newspapers

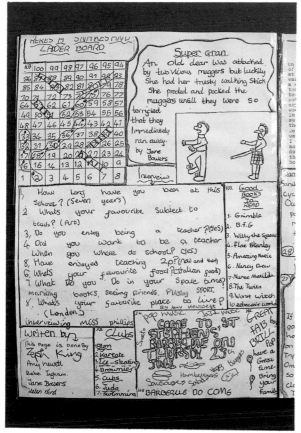

DISCUSSION:

Why do we have newspapers?

The different newspapers available — including free newspapers.

How can newspapers be free?

A newspaper contains 'news'. What else does it contain?

Compare the same news story in different newspapers.

Can you believe anything you read in newspapers?

LANGUAGE:

Writing:

- Write a newspaper report on a particular event restricting the report to between 180 to 200 words. Include an appropriate headline.
- Supply the story for a given headline. E.g. "Turning the Tables".
- Write newspaper reports on historical events as a reporter of the day.
- Write a report on a school event or a local issue for the local newspaper, and send it with a covering letter to the editor.

Research:

How many copies of the major national newspapers are sold each day? Find out about: Newsagency, Reuters, Oxford Gazette, London Gazette, proof reading, Fleet Street.

Drama/Movement:

- *The Interview.* Act out a scene in which a newspaper reporter interviews a particularly difficult member of the public in an effort to gather details for a story.
- A story becomes dramatically changed when it is passed on by a number of people.

Vocabulary:
Newsagent, editor, articles, column, headline, caption, reporter, news-stand, newsprint, journalist, tabloid, pulp, newshawk, newshound, newsmonger, news-sheet, newsworthy, reviews, advertisement, bulletin, publicity, deadline, distribution, media.

Stories:
Emil and the Detectives, E. Kastner, Puffin.
The Cartoonist, Betsy Byars, Puffin.

Poetry:
'News is conveyed by letter word or mouth,
and comes to us from North, East, West or South', from *Witt's Recreation*.

MATHEMATICS:

A study of the weather section in a national newspaper — comparison of temperatures in different countries, graphs of maximum temperatures, hours of sunshine.

The area of paper available for printing in a newspaper, and the area taken up for different purposes, e.g. photographs, T.V., sport, advertisements. Record your results as a graph.

The cost per year of purchasing different newspapers.

Are all crossword designs symmetrical? Do they have rotational symmetry?

How much does a sheet of newspaper weigh?

Approximately how many words in a newspaper? Devise a method for calculating this.

How many sheets of a particular newspaper would be needed to cover the classroom floor?

Which typewriter key on the editor's typewriter is likely to wear out first? Investigate.

Investigate the different ways numbers are used in a newspaper.

Make a collection of headlines which include numbers.

SCIENCE, DESIGN & TECHNOLOGY:

'It is easy to tear newsprint in straight lines in one direction and not in another' — investigate.

Make a boat from one sheet of newspaper — how long can your boat support 20 gram weights before sinking or tipping?

Devise a test for comparing the absorption properties of newsprint with other types of paper.

Make your own paper.

Make a self-supporting tower out of one sheet of newspaper. Who can construct the tallest tower?

ART/CRAFT:

Papier mâché work.

A study of printing techniques.

Make pictures using only dots, as in a newspaper photograph.

Design and draw an advert of given dimensions for a particular product.

Design and produce a cartoon strip story.

Newspaper montage.

Make hats from newspapers.

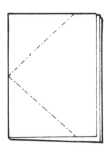 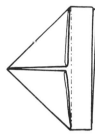 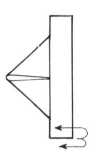 

COMPUTER PROGRAMS:

Use desk-top publishing or view data programs to produce a class or school newspaper
View (Software Production Associates)
Front Page (MAPE TAPE 2)
Front Page Extra (MAPE TAPE 3)
News Bulletin (MAPE TAPE 4)
Typesetter and *The Fleet Street Phantom* (Sherston Software)
Newsagent (R.E.S.O.U.R.C.E.)
Fleet Street Editor (Mirrorsoft)
Newspaper (SPA)
Scoop (British Telecom Education Service)

ENVIRONMENTAL STUDIES:

The development of newspapers.
Create a class broadsheet or newspaper reporting on school events –
children should take on the various jobs such as editor, photographer,
reporter, etc.
Study advertisements in your local newspaper and comment on their
effectiveness.
The Newspaper from tree to breakfast table.
A wall frieze can be developed showing the stages from paper making
through obtaining copy, collating, printing and delivery to reading.
Visit your library to study old local newspapers – discover what was
happening in your area, (a) 25 years ago, (b) 50 years ago.
Try to study a copy of a newspaper printed on the day you were born.
Find out about the jobs of an editor, a reporter, a newspaper
photographer, a compositor, and a journalist – taking notes, taping
interviews, verifying facts, typing and word-processing skills.
A study of weather reports.
Recycling newsprint – conservation.

TOYS/GAMES:	*Newsreader,* E.J. Arnold & Son Ltd.

TOYS/GAMES: *Newsreader,* E.J. Arnold & Son Ltd.
Who can tear the longest unbroken strip from a sheet of newspaper?
Crosswords — design and compose crosswords.
Make a collection of games and puzzles found in newspapers, and put forward some new ideas for a newspaper puzzle page.

VISITS: The local newsagent.
The local newspaper office.
Invite a newspaper reporter, photographer or editor to visit the school.
Paper-making factory.

OTHER AREAS FOR DISCUSSION AND INVESTIGATION: When were the different national newspapers first produced and how did they obtain their names?
Use *The Guinness Book of Records* to discover:-
    (a) The oldest existing newspaper in the world.
    (b) The earliest British newspaper.
    (c) The largest and smallest newspapers ever printed.
    (d) The highest circulation for a newspaper.
Type sizes and how they are measured.
Collect as many different newspaper titles as possible, and categorise them as daily, weekly, local, regional, national, foreign, evening, Sunday, etc.
Discuss colour printing in newspapers.
What's black and white and read all over?
Make a collection of newspapers from other countries.

string and rope

DISCUSSION: The different uses for string and rope.
What is the difference between string and rope?
Ways of using string or rope for emergencies.
Different types of string and ropes.
Describe how to tie a particular knot.
How long is a piece of string?

LANGUAGE: **Writing:**
- *The rope that saved a life.*
- Write a play to be acted by string puppets.
- **Can you write a word-string in an interesting shape?**

Can you write a word-string in an interesting shape?

Research:
Find out about:- rope ladder, string of pearls, rope dance, tight rope, rope walk, tow rope, bowstring, cat gut, stringed instruments, string of horses, string quartet, Turk's head, guy rope, string tie, cat's cradle, hamstring, Indian rope trick.

Drama/Movement:
- Mime – two people attached by an imaginary piece of rope.
- Act out the story of *Theseus and the Minotaur* (trad.)
- String puppet plays.

Vocabulary:
Twine, sisal, strand, yarn, fibre, splice, sheet, stay, fray, hemp, stringy, cord, stringent, ligature, hawser, painter, halyard, lanyard, halter, noose.

Word strings:
ANVIL, ILLUMINATE, TEARFUL, ULTRAMARINE – (ANVILLUMINATEARFULTRAMARINE)

Phrases and Sayings:
Give him enough rope to hang himself, give someone plenty of rope, know the ropes, ropey (slang), to rope in, highly-strung, string along, no strings attached, hamstrung, second string (competitor), strings to your bow, pulling the strings, without strings, string along, string together.

Stories:
Mountaineering stories.
Theseus and the Minotaur, Greek Myth.

Poetry:
'Henry King (who chewed bits of string)', Hilaire Belloc, in *Selected Cautionary Verses,* Puffin.
'A Rope for Harry Fat', by James K. Baxter, in *Ballads Old and New,* Hutton.
'Skipping Song', by John Walsh in *Oxford Books of Verse for Juniors, Book 2,* OUP.

MATHEMATICS:

Use string to determine the longer of two wiggly lines.

Use string to estimate distances on a map.

Use string and a weight to make and investigate pendulums of different lengths.

Use a plumb line to find vertical surfaces.

Use two drawing pins and a loop of string to draw an ellipse:

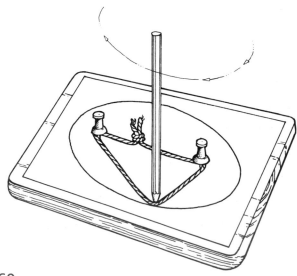

Threading and lacing patterns.

Investigate the lengths of string required to tie cuboid-shaped parcels of different dimensions.

SCIENCE, DESIGN & TECHNOLOGY:
Lift weights using rope and pulleys.

Make a study of wave patterns transmitted along a length of rope.

Design and make some camping gadgets using wood and rope.

Use string and tins to make a telephone.

Devise a strength test for cotton, threads and string.

Investigate the sound properties of different kinds, lengths, thicknesses and tautness of strings.

Devise a method for rolling a length of string into a ball.

Use string and effective supports to make a model of a rope bridge or a telepherique (aerial cable car).

String an old badminton or tennis racquet.

Demonstrate centrifugal force — attach weights securely. **Swing small weight in a circle. Large weight is raised. Keep children well away!**

ART/CRAFT:
Study the effects of water on rope and knots; the implications for mooring boats, pitching tents, etc.

Mount samples of different knots on a display board.

Make string puppets.

String collage — string can be dipped into different coloured paints before glueing to card.

String sculpture; macramé; weaving; mobiles.

Tie-dye.

String painting — dip string in paint and pull between two sheets of paper.

String printing.

Make a holder for a ball of string.

COMPUTER PROGRAM:
Quilts (Microsmile 2 — The Next 17) (MEP)

MUSIC:
'Puppet on a String', Bill Martin and Phil Coulter.
'String of Pearls', Glen Miller.
Skipping Songs, e.g. 'Skip to my Lou'.
Make a list of stringed instruments.
Study the inside of a piano.

ENVIRONMENTAL STUDIES:
A study of different knots and their uses — include: reef knot, sheet bend, clove hitch, sheep shank, bowline and the highwayman's hitch for tying up a horse ready for a quick getaway
Cat-o'-nine tails: sailors made one as a punishment on board ship before being flogged.
A study of ship's rigging.
Mooring a boat.
Fishing nets and sports nets.
How are string and rope made? What are they made of?

P.E./GAMES:
A variety of skipping activities.
Climbing ropes and rope ladders.
Tug o'War.
Rope jump — children stand in a circle and jump weighted rope swung by teacher.

TOYS/GAMES:
The gyroscope.
Spinning top and whip.
Kites.
Newton's Cradle.
Cat's cradle and other string games — (*Cat's Cradle and Other String Games*, Camilla Gryski, Angus & Robertson Publishers.)

VISITS:
Rope makers.
A person with naval connections could demonstrate various knots and splices.
A conjuror could perform rope and string tricks.
Local boatyard.

OTHER AREAS FOR DISCUSSION AND INVESTIGATION:
Use *The Guinness Book of Records* to discover the largest ball of string ever made, and the largest stringed instrument ever constructed.
Investigate the advantages of nylon rope.
How ropes are used by mountaineers.
Ropes can whip, but how do you whip a rope? (with twine, to stop the end fraying).
Make and display a collection of as many different types of string and rope as possible.
'String Rope and Knot Problems' — see *Sources of Mathematical Discovery* and *Investigations in Mathematics* by Lorraine Mottershead, Basil Blackwell.
Brain Boosters by David Webster, Pan Books.
The Book of Experiments, and *The Second Book of Experiments*, Leonard de Vries, John Murray.

telephones

DISCUSSION:
List as many forms of communication as possible.
Consider for which purposes the telephone is the most appropriate.
Communication before the telephone.
How is the telephone central to the work of — a doctor, journalist, air pilot, school secretary, etc?
What effect does the telephone have on the lives of the children?

LANGUAGE:

Writing:
- *The call that changed my life.*
- Write about a burglar who is caught after dropping a list of telephone numbers.
- *Dial 999.*
- Telephone-time costs money. Plan a 1-minute telephone call to a distant cousin giving as much information about your school as possible.
- Plan an instruction sheet for a telephone box explaining how the phone should be used.

Research:
Find out what you can about cordless telephones, car telephones, push-button phones, satellite calls, STD calls, reverse-charge calls, free-fone calls, personal calls, video-phones, answerphones, modems, the telephone alphabet.

63

Drama/Movement:
- *Crossed-line* sketches.
- Act out an emergency ('999' call) story.
- Devise a humorous sketch in which 2 telephones converse about the people who use them.
- Sit two pupils back-to-back and make imaginary phone calls between e.g. dentist and patient, borrower and lender, policeman and suspect (Conversations can be taped and their clarity and effectiveness discussed).

Vocabulary:
- Exchange, dial, switchboard, directory, code, international, operator, receiver, cable, etc.
- Derivation of the word 'telephone'.
- Find other words beginning with 'tele-' or containing 'phone'.
- What is a telepheme?
- A telestich is a poem or block of words whose final letters spell a name or a word (c.f. acrostic). Write a verse or a passage as a telestich. Try to make it relevant to the subject of the telephone.

Stories:
Make use of the BT Bedtime Storyline Service.
'Telephone Travel' — story by Richard Hughes in *The Spider's Palace*, Puffin.

Poetry:
'Telegraph Poles', by Paul Dehn, in *My Kind of Verse*, Burke Books.
'Think of 8 numbers', Shelley Silverstein in *Beastly Boys and Ghastly Girls*, Methuen.

MATHEMATICS:

Investigate telephone charges. Set some practical problems using the scale of charges given in the directory.

Note the special costs of personal and reverse-charge calls.

Telephone Bills — rental charges and unit costs.

How many different 2, 3, 4-figure numbers can be dialled? If appropriate, extend this investigation to longer numbers. A separate survey can be made of palindromic numbers.

Time differences. If you ring someone at, say 7pm, what time will it be in various other countries? The code book time-zone may be useful.

Devise a memory test. How many consecutive digits can be remembered after different time intervals? Results can be tabulated and recorded in graphical form.

SCIENCE, DESIGN & TECHNOLOGY:

Make a simple communicator by attaching (a) tins at the ends of a length of string: (b) funnels at the ends of a length of tube.

Find out how a telephone works.

Design an easy-reference telephone directory other than in book form. (e.g. a flip-card system).

Design an alternative to the telephone bell ringing system.

Invent an instrument which would aid a person who does not have full use of his/her hands to dial a telephone number.

ART/CRAFT:
Design and draw an advert which would encourage people to use the telephone more often.

Design a telephone for the future. What other features could be usefully incorporated?

Make a wall time-frieze of pictures showing the development of methods of sending messages, e.g. bonfires, smoke-signals, heliograph, semaphore tower, ship flag signals, telephone, communications satellite, modem, etc.

COMPUTER PROGRAMS:
It is possible for schools to communicate with each other via the computer using a modem telephone link. Explore the possibilities using the Times Network Systems (TTNS).
The Magic Telephone (MAPE TAPE 4)
Phonin (Primary Programs Ltd.)

MUSIC:
Make use of the telephone service 'Discline'.
Compose a piece of music which can be played over the telephone while someone is waiting to be connected.

ENVIRONMENTAL STUDIES:
The development of telecommunications.
Inventors — e.g. Bell, Edison.
Use the Yellow Pages or a local directory to find out who can be contacted to provide the following services:- plumber, takeaway meal, car hire, pest control, chemist, chimney sweep, model shop, travel agent, roof-repairer, etc.
Locate the public telephones in your area. Mark them, together with their numbers, on a local map.
Make a study of your local Emergency Services (include cave, coast and mountain rescue if applicable, as well as police, fire, and ambulance).
Why was *999* selected as the emergency call number?
Using an old telephone, practise making emergency calls with the teacher acting as the operator.
Investigate the many different telephone information services.
Find out about underwater cable-laying ships (e.g. 'The Great Eastern') and trench digging machines like 'Sea dog'.
Find out about a telephonist's job. Perhaps opportunities can be found for pupils to answer the school office phone.

VISIT:
Local telephone exchange or the switchboard of a large office.
The Science Museum.

OTHER AREAS FOR DISCUSSION AND INVESTIGATION:

Use *The Guinness Book of Records* to find out:-
  (a) Which country has the greatest length of telephone lines?
  (b) The length of the longest telephone cable.
  (c) Where is the world's largest switchboard?

Find out about telephone cards. Where can they be bought? How are they used?

Suggest other services which might be provided by the telephone companies. Develop and produce some of your ideas.

Investigate the different telephone tones:- dialling, ringing, engaged, number unobtainable, payline, foreign.

List the telephone exchange codes of major cities.

Find out and memorise your local exchange codes.

Prepare a list of telephone numbers important to you. Remember to include local services which you might need to use.

Use the telephone directory for alphabetical order exercises and speed games.

'E.T. . . .Phone Home!'

Some notes on the use of the computer in Project Studies:

The study of most topics can be enhanced by use of the computer. Whilst it may be possible to find programs which will be directly relevant to a theme being studied, we wish to emphasise the benefit to all project studies of the following range of open-ended programs, where the content and application can be controlled by the teacher and/or the children:-

1. Data-handling programs such as FACTFILE and PICFILE (C.U.P.), QUEST (AUCBE), GRASS (Newman College), SUPASTORE DATABASE (ESM) and KEY (ITV) can be used for examining and interrogating data collected in the course of project investigations.
2. The use of a word-processing package will stimulate interest and provide clearly produced written work related to the project being studied. Such software will also be invaluable in the production of worksheets, questionnaires and reports. Some of the programs found to be most useful with primary school children are:- EDWORD (Clwyd Technics Ltd), WORDWISE (Computer Concepts Ltd), WRITER (MEP Primary Project), WRITE (Oxfordshire CC), MICKEY (Northants CEC), PENDOWN (Logotron Ltd), FOLIO (Tedimen Software), PROMPT (MEP Bluefile).
3. Desk-top Publishing programs such as NEWSPAPER (SPA), FLEET STREET EDITOR (Mirrorsoft) and viewdata systems such as VIEW (SPA) will enable the results of topic work to be produced as leaflets, news-sheets or magazines.
4. Topic-related information can be investigated at a level appropriate to the language skills of the class using teacher-prepared passages with language prediction programs such as TRAY (MEP) and JUNCLOZE (MAPE TAPE 2).
5. Those schools which have a computer with a modem link will be able to make use of the facilities offered by The Times Network Systems (TTNS), the National Educational Resources Information Service (NERIS) and/or PRESTEL. In particular, the opportunities for collecting information and exchanging data with other schools, for communicating by means of electronic mail and for investigating large databases will considerably extend the possibilities for developing project studies.

ADDITIONAL NOTES AND REFERENCES
Balloons

Bicycles

Bottles

Boxes

Bricks

Clocks

Footwear

Hats and Headgear

Ladders

Letters

Mirrors

Money

Newspaper

String and Rope

Telephones

For details of other Belair Publications
please write to:
Belair Publications Ltd.,
P.O. Box 12
TWICKENHAM TW1 2QL, England.